HOW TO BE
PERFECTLY
imperfect

STOP COMPARING, START LIVING

CANDI WILLIAMS

HOW TO BE PERFECTLY IMPERFECT

An Hachette UK Company
www.hachette.co.uk

Vie Books, an imprint of Summersdale Publishers Ltd
Part of Octopus Publishing Group Limited
Carmelite House
50 Victoria Embankment
LONDON
EC4Y 0DZ
UK

www.summersdale.com

Printed and bound in the Czech Republic

ISBN: 978-1-78783-234-3

Substantial discounts on bulk quantities of Summersdale books are available to corporations, professional associations and other organizations. For details contact general enquiries: telephone: +44 (0) 1243 771107 or email: enquiries@summersdale.com.

CONTENTS

Introduction

You were not put on this earth to be perfect.
You were put on this earth to be you.

This little book is here to show you that, despite all
those insta-images, media messages and tiring thought
patterns, you are good enough exactly as you are.
You do not need to change a single thing about
yourself to meet someone else's definition of perfect.

Perfect doesn't equal happy. In fact, the best way
to be happy is to stop trying to be perfect.

So get ready to let go of those feelings of not being
good enough, the "I'll be happy when _____" messages
and worrying about what other people think. It's
time to start living and loving yourself a bit more.

Part one:

The problem with perfectionism

One of the big problems with perfectionism is that it often disguises itself as ambition, drive and motivation. All of those things can be good. It's good to strive for something. It's good to have dreams, to work hard to achieve. But these traits can fast become obsessive, all-consuming and unattainable.

Perfectionism has a wicked way of imposing impossible-to-reach standards upon us. Often when we meet one of the standards, another one pops right up to try us – kind of like the game Whac-A-Mole. And just like trying to hit faux moles at record pace, perfectionism can be exhausting.

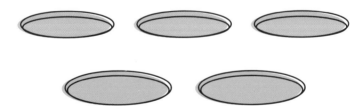

perfectionism

noun

constantly striving to achieve unrealistic
goals or meet unattainable standards; seeing
anything less than flawlessness as self-failure

We are
born to
be real,
not to be
perfect.

DON'T AIM FOR *PERFECTION.* AIM FOR "*BETTER THAN YESTERDAY*".

Izey Victoria Odiase

Stop should-ing and never-ing yourself

"I'll never be good enough."

"I must lose weight."

Sound familiar? The problem is that using words like *never, always, must* and *should* sets unrealistic expectations for us to adhere to certain standards.

The truth is: we're human! *Sometimes,* we make mistakes, we indulge or we don't feel our best – because we're real.

So give yourself a break and start swapping out your *should*s for *could*s and *always* for *sometimes*, e.g.

- *Sometimes,* I feel like I'm not good enough but I have plenty of friends who love me for who I am.

- I *could* go to the gym but if I'm not feeling up to it, I *could* also do a workout at home.

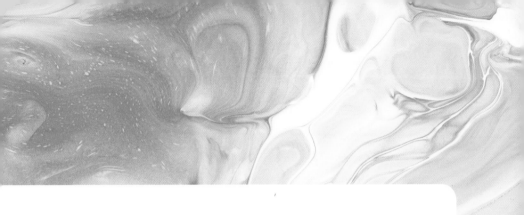

Recognize perfectionism

There's no "one size fits all" when it comes to perfectionism. In fact, a study by Danielle S. Molnar identified three types of perfectionism:

- Self-oriented perfectionism – where individuals impose high standards on themselves.

- Socially prescribed perfectionism – where individuals feel that others expect them to be perfect.

- Other-oriented perfectionism – where individuals place high standards upon others.

These different elements of perfectionism can appear together or on their own. Understanding them can help you notice when they pop up in your day-to-day life. Rather than seeing the high standards you put on yourself/others as essential, see it for what it is – perfectionism creeping up on you.

You are not a robot

Remember, you are human – beautifully, uniquely human.
And just like all other humans, you have limits, flaws and
needs. Rest and self-care are just as important as food
and water so instead of piling the pressure on yourself,
recognize your limits and take time to slow down.

Think:

- Is this realistic?

- What are my stress levels like right now?

- How can I break this down into
  something more achievable?

- What's the actual impact of me reaching
  good enough but not perfect here?

The toxic side of perfectionism

Perfectionism can often be confused with motivation and touted as a positive thing but, in actual fact, it's linked to a whole list of health issues, including:

- Anxiety

- Depression

- Eating disorders

- High blood pressure

- Bipolar disorder

Now, that's not to say that if you're a perfectionist then you'll suffer from these conditions, but it does highlight that perfectionism is stressful and that it can have a real impact on our health and well-being.

Loosening the grip of perfectionism

Perfectionism can take a pretty tight hold – especially if it's always been a feature in your life. Here are a few signs that you might be suffering from perfectionism:

- You're super hard on yourself. You work hard to give 110 per cent in all that you do and if you don't meet your expectations, you beat yourself up about it.

- Criticism cuts deep. Negative feedback hurts you as it makes you feel imperfect.

- Everything's got to be "just right". You like everything to be done perfectly or what's the point?

- You obsess about mistakes. Even when the tiniest thing goes wrong, it feels huge to you and you struggle to stop thinking about it.

IN A WORLD WHERE EVERYONE IS SEARCHING FOR PERFECTION,

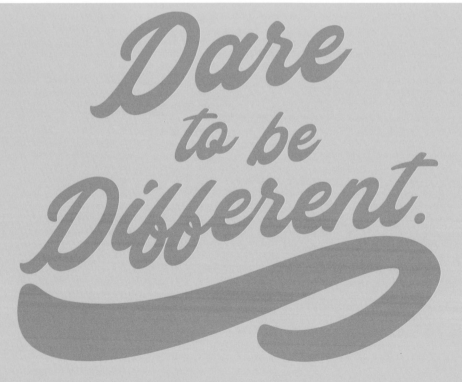

Dare to be Different.

Acknowledge that perfectionism isn't good for you

It can be really, really difficult trying to be absolutely amazing at everything you do. If you want to shake off perfectionism, firstly you need to acknowledge it's not good for you.

Just like smoking or too much alcohol, researchers are all in agreement that perfectionism can be highly detrimental to your health. When you notice it's getting too much, pause, re-prioritize and put your well-being top of your to-do list.

PERFECTIONISM

IS A

DANGEROUS

STATE OF MIND IN AN

IMPERFECT WORLD.

Robert Hillyer

What's the worst that can happen?

Think about it: what would actually happen if something you did wasn't quite perfect? Chances are the world won't set alight and your loved ones won't all turn against you. Don't believe me? Give it a go. Try it with something with low-level risk – like sending an email to a workmate without proofreading it, going out without brushing your hair or buying something without reading every single review ever first. At first, it might seem totally unnatural but it'll help you see that you really, really don't have to be perfect at absolutely everything.

Perfectionist thinking traps

Perfectionism can filter how you think. Understanding some of these thinking patterns can help you stop falling into their unhelpful traps. Examples of perfectionist thinking patterns:

- Black-and-white thinking: "It's all or nothing." This thinking pattern focuses on either being absolutely perfect or a complete failure – with no in between.

- Catastrophic thinking: "It'll be the end of the world if I don't..." Catastrophic thinking does what it says on the tin – it magnifies the impact of even the smallest events and distorts reality with worst-case scenarios.

Overcoming perfectionist thinking traps

The first step is recognizing these unhelpful thinking patterns. The second step is challenging them! So when you notice these thinking patterns creeping in, use the following questions to get a more balanced perspective:

- Is this a thought or a fact?

- What evidence do I have that this is true? What evidence do I have that it isn't?

- Am I 100 per cent sure that this will happen?

- How many times has this happened before?

- Is it so important that my future depends on it?

- Will I care about this in ten days, ten months or ten years?

- What is the worst that could happen?

- If it did happen, what could I do to cope with or handle it?

- Am I confusing "possibility" with "certainty"? It may be possible, but how likely is it?

If you look for perfection, you'll never be content.

Leo Tolstoy

REMEMBER:
THERE'S SO MUCH
MORE TO LIFE
THAN LIKES.

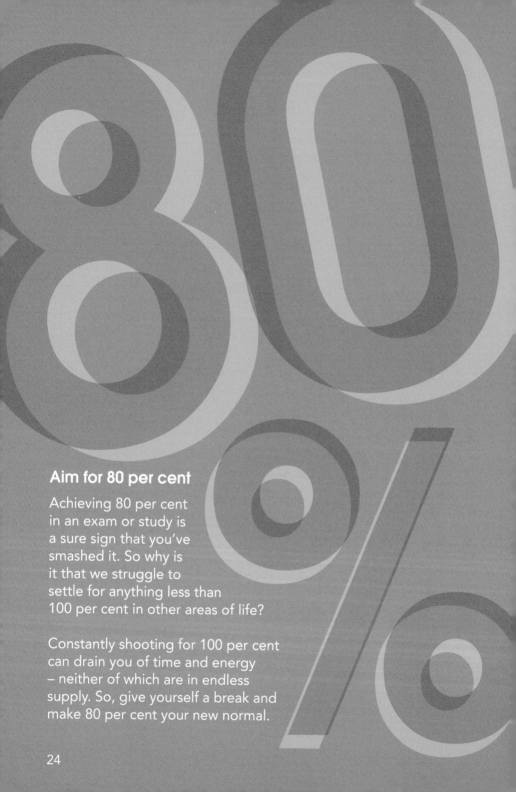

Aim for 80 per cent

Achieving 80 per cent in an exam or study is a sure sign that you've smashed it. So why is it that we struggle to settle for anything less than 100 per cent in other areas of life?

Constantly shooting for 100 per cent can drain you of time and energy – neither of which are in endless supply. So, give yourself a break and make 80 per cent your new normal.

IT IS ALWAYS ENOUGH TO HAVE DONE YOUR BEST.

DEMOTE YOUR INNER PERFECTIONIST.

Selena Rezvani

Understand the difference between striving and straining

Striving to achieve a goal isn't a bad thing. But there's a huge difference between striving for something achievable and straining for things to be perfect.

Think of it like this:

Striving: when you're already content with who you are, but you recognize something that you could be even better at – and you set out to achieve this in a healthy way.

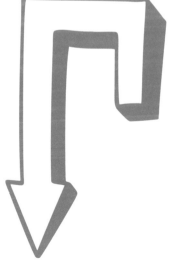

Straining: this comes from a place of feeling inferior, or less than, and believing that you need to achieve X, Y or Z to like or love yourself.

Are you striving or straining?

Striving should feel positive. It's all about setting realistic goals, achieving your potential and doing it in a healthy way, where you enjoy the process, not just the outcome.

Straining, on the other hand, epitomizes perfectionism and can put huge pressure on you to meet impossible standards. Here are a few tips to help you recognize and overcome the strain:

- Watch out for words like *need*, *must* and *have to* – striving for goals should be enjoyable not a chore!

- Is it really achievable? If not, why are you doing it? You might be amazing but you're not superhuman.

- Are you meeting your standards or someone else's? Yours are really the only ones that truly matter.

REPEAT THREE
TIMES A DAY:

"I AM WORTHY.
I AM WHOLE.
MY WORTH DOES
NOT DEPEND ON
MY JOB/LOOKS/
PRODUCTIVITY."

PERFECTION IS JUST BORING... WHAT'S NATURAL OR REAL; THAT IS BEAUTY.

Marc Jacobs

REMEMBER: OTHER PEOPLE'S OPINIONS DON'T CHANGE YOUR AWESOMENESS.

Break it down now

Often, goals can be unrealistic objectives in disguise.
To see if your goal is achievable, try breaking it down into
mini goals. Give it a go using the format below and try
to make them as granular as possible – your mini goals
should read like step-by-step tasks that get you to your
bigger goal. If you end up with loads of them, ask yourself
how achievable it really is. Are you striving or straining?

goal

I want to:

_____
_____
_____
_____
_____
_____
_____
_____
_____
_____
_____
_____
_____

mini goals

So I'm going to:

_____
_____
_____
_____
_____
_____
_____
_____
_____

Grow in your own time peacefully.

Chidera Eggerue

Separate the must-haves
from the nice-to-haves

As much as I'd like to marry a movie star and live happily ever after on a paradise island, it's not the be-all and end-all if I don't. A good tip for coping with the pressures of perfectionism is separating the must-haves from the nice-to-haves.

Take looking for a new house. Some of your must-haves might be:

- A bedroom with room for all your stuff
- A manageable amount of work required
- Some garden space to relax in the summer
- A safe neighbourhood

Your nice-to-haves, on the other hand, could be:

- Room for a hot tub

- A driveway with space for two cars

- Five acres of land for that swimming pool
  you might get in five years' time

- A fireplace like the one in Hogwarts so
  you can pretend you're a wizard

Perfectionists often tend to group the nice-to-haves
with the must-haves, which goes back to those
unrelentingly high standards. By separating them out,
you can assess what's really achievable and what's not.
Are your must-haves good enough for right now?

Be happy with being you.

Love your flaws.

Own your quirks.

And know that you are just

as perfect as anyone else.

exactly as you are.

Ariana Grande

Focus on a growth mindset

Life isn't a pass or fail exercise. Things are
constantly changing, shifting and evolving so
it's important that our mindsets reflect this.

Fixed mindsets tend to see things as black and white,
perfect or rubbish. Growth mindsets, on the other hand,
are more flexible. They put the focus on trying and
learning rather than winning or losing. Take driving a
car for instance: you don't drive perfectly the first time
you get behind the wheel; you learn from mistakes
and build up your ability. Life is no different – it's a
constant learning journey – so focus on how you grow
and improve along the way, not just the destination.

Your thoughts are not facts.

Own your
thoughts and
don't take any
sh*t from your
inner critic.

Start small

One of the other downsides of perfectionism is that we place such high expectations on ourselves that we don't know where to start! This can result in the dreaded pit of procrastination. But things always seem impossible until they're done so when you find yourself putting something off, start small. Even if it's just for five minutes, start chipping away. You'll feel much better for it.

You, yourself, as much as anybody
in the entire universe, deserve
your love and affection.

Sharon Salzberg

Start learning self-love

You weren't born a perfectionist; it's something that's been triggered by past experiences and thought patterns. The good news is that just as you've learned to be hard on yourself over the years, you can learn to be kinder to yourself. Hoorah!

You can train your brain in self-compassion in a number of ways.

❶ Check in with yourself. Often we're so busy doing the do that we don't stop to think about how we're feeling or what we need. So, start taking the time to check in with yourself and focus on what you need right now, rather than just what's on your to-do list.

❷ Forgive yourself. If you're anything like me, you'll have wasted hours and hours of your life overanalyzing your mistakes. But it's a waste of time and energy. Learn from them, forgive yourself and move on.

❸ Remember that life is unpredictable. It's hard to be perfect in an imperfect world. Life is full of ebbs and flows, peaks and troughs and you're just trying to find your way along the bumpy road. So, go easy on yourself. Allow for detours, plans to change and mountains to climb. It's a marathon not a sprint.

STRIVE
FOR
PROGRESS,
NOT
PERFECTION.

Don't let your inner bully knock you down

Notice your self-talk when you're giving yourself a hard time – you know that voice that pops up and says horrible things when you're feeling fragile.

- Look out for "I am" phrases and make sure you're not giving yourself lots of negative labels like "I am fat" or "I am ugly" – try to replace these with more positive ones like "I am doing my best" and "I am a good person".

- Distract your inner critic. Actively try to overcome your negative thoughts by thinking about something more positive. Disney films, Beyoncé songs, types of cheese – the choice is yours.

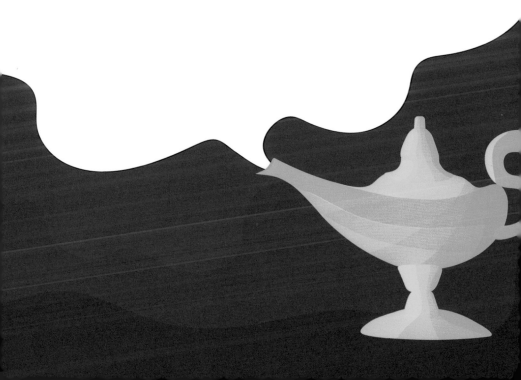

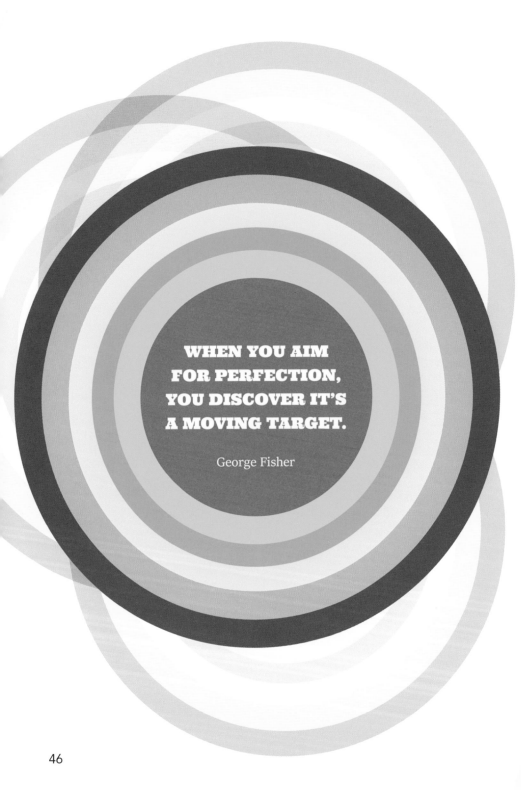

WHEN YOU AIM FOR PERFECTION, YOU DISCOVER IT'S A MOVING TARGET.

George Fisher

Ask for help more

Another trait of perfectionism is believing that you have to manage everything on your own. Not only is that exhausting but it's often pretty unachievable.

There is no shame whatsoever in asking for help. In fact, I'd encourage you to do it more. Let people in. Whether it's asking a friend for advice, delegating something at work or speaking to a professional, don't ever be afraid to ask for help. You can't do it all and no one expects you to.

Part Two:

Overcoming that feeling of not being good enough

How many times have you found yourself feeling like you're not good enough?

No matter what you do or achieve, the "not good enough" demon can leave you feeling like a failure.

So, over the next chapter, we'll unpack the what, why and how of your inner critic and look at all the reasons why you are absolutely, totally, beautifully good enough.

We can feel
negative emotions
three times more
strongly than
positive ones
(so never let anyone
tell you you're being
oversensitive).

Why do we always feel like we're not good enough?

Not feeling good enough is in our very nature as human beings. Lots of it is rooted in our brain's "negativity bias". In psychological terms, this means that things of a negative nature have a greater effect on our psychological state than neutral or positive ones.

In simple terms, that means that our brains are wired to give more weight to the bad stuff than the good. Back in our hunter-gatherer days, this helped keep us super alert to dangers, like a bear running toward us, but nowadays when bad news is just a click or flick of the TV channel away, it can cause us problems and have a negative impact on our self-esteem. Our negativity bias explains why we shrug off the nice things people say, but if someone reads our text and doesn't reply, our brains can go into overdrive and start thinking the worst.

Our clever minds even have their own in-built alarm bell, called the amygdala, that constantly scans for bad news and files it away. It's also the same part of our brain that's responsible for our emotions so you can start to see why sometimes we end up feeling less than perfect and not good enough.

Thankfully, by understanding this, we can start to change it.

Managing our brain's alarm bells

Just as we do with our morning alarm bells,
we can take control of our brain's alarm
bells too. Stacks of psychological research
has found that we're able to challenge our
negative thinking to help us stop ending up
in a pit of insecurity, sadness and anxiety.

How? By starting to change the way we
interpret information and experiences.
The handy tips over the next pages are
designed to help you do just that.

Start taking notice of the good things – even if they seem small

Before bed, write down everything that went well that day and what you're grateful for. I find this so powerful. It's so easy to finish a day thinking "today was rubbish", but every time I've challenged myself to write down what went well, I've been surprised at how many little positives I've found. It's a good way of reminding yourself that although things might not be perfect, there's still good to be found in every day.

I AM NOT ENOUGH.

INSTEAD OF
NOTICING
FLAWS,
START
NOTICING
THOSE
THINGS YOU
LOVE ABOUT
YOURSELF.

Break the negative pattern

Negative thoughts can go from zero to 100 real quick.
You know how it is: one bad thing happens and
before you know it, your life feels like it's over, you're
crying into packets of unhealthy snacks and Netflix
is taunting you by asking if you're still watching.

To break the spiral, distract yourself when the negative
thoughts start to crop up. Put your full focus into something
else like reading a book, tidying up or going to the gym.
Putting a wash on is my go-to – not the most glamorous,
but it works – and you get a sense of achievement too!

AT THE END OF THE DAY,
REMIND YOURSELF THAT YOU DID
THE BEST YOU COULD TODAY,

and

that

is

good

enough.

Lori Deschene

Would you say that to a friend?

We can be so cruel to ourselves when
we're not feeling good enough.

Next time negative thoughts creep in, ask yourself how
you'd react to someone else going through that situation.

What advice would you give them? How would you
support them? Would you call them stupid and tell them
it's typical or would you show them kindness and help
them to feel better, not worse? Mirror that with how you
treat yourself. Be gentle and show yourself compassion,
rather than kicking yourself when you're already down.

Instead of this	_Try this_
"Things always go wrong for me."	"Okay, so that didn't go so well but who doesn't make mistakes every now and then? What can I learn for next time?"
"I don't feel good about myself."	"There must be some things I like about myself. My eyes? My creativity? My kind heart? I'm going to pick out my good qualities and write them down."
"I wish I looked like that."	"That person looks great but that's not me. I have my own unique body, face, style and personality, and so do they. I can work on being my best self without wishing to be someone else."
"I'm rubbish at it."	"So what? I'm not good at this one thing, but I'm good at a whole host of other things."

THERE ARE ALMOST EIGHT BILLION PEOPLE
IN THIS WORLD – EACH AND EVERY ONE OF
THEM HAS STRENGTHS AND WEAKNESSES.

NOBODY'S PERFECT.

See setbacks as lessons

It's pretty inevitable that things won't always go perfectly in life, but focusing on the downsides of every situation will only make you feel worse. Instead of thinking what went wrong, think: What lesson is this trying to teach me?

For instance if you're beating yourself up about falling out with a friend or something going wrong at work, think about how else you could have approached it. Are there any positives of the situation? Reframing the way you think about things can help you uncover more constructive, useful perspectives.

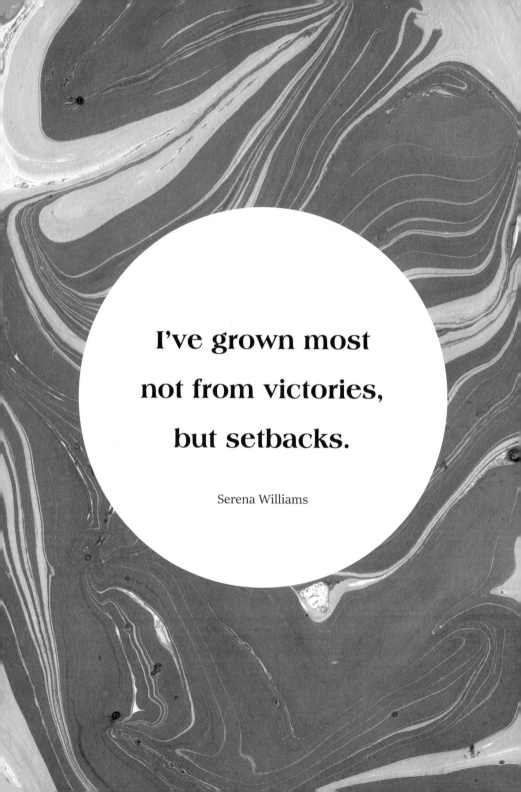

I've grown most
not from victories,
but setbacks.

Serena Williams

Feel fabulous

Apparently, we look in the mirror eight times a day – add that to all the times we check ourselves out in car windows or on our phone screens and it's safe to say we're an appearance-conscious bunch. For many of us, it's something we obsess about. But there's so much more to life than just how we look. What matters more is how we feel.

So instead of stressing about looking good,
start obsessing about feeling good.

Not sure where to start? Here's some feel-good inspiration:

Enjoy a home spa

Certain essential oils – like bergamot, mandarin and lavender – are known for their mood-lifting powers. Pop five to ten drops in a bath, oil burner or diffuser and r-e-l-a-x!

Work it out

Exercise releases all kinds of feel-great hormones. Even if it's just a 15-minute home workout, introduce some more movement into your week and enjoy the boost it gives you.

Do a power dance

Dancing is a great way to feel good pretty instantly. So put some guilty pleasures on and cut a few shapes around your room – now tell me you don't feel better?

Find the exception to the rule

It's really hard to think positively when you're stuck in a whirlwind of negative thoughts. So start by trying to find just one exception to the narrative your inner critic is taunting you with.

For instance, when my narrative is telling me I'm unlovable over and over again, an exception to the rule could be that I've been loved and have friends and family who love me.

Start to challenge your inner critic and show it who's boss!

Love

your

body,

unapologetically.

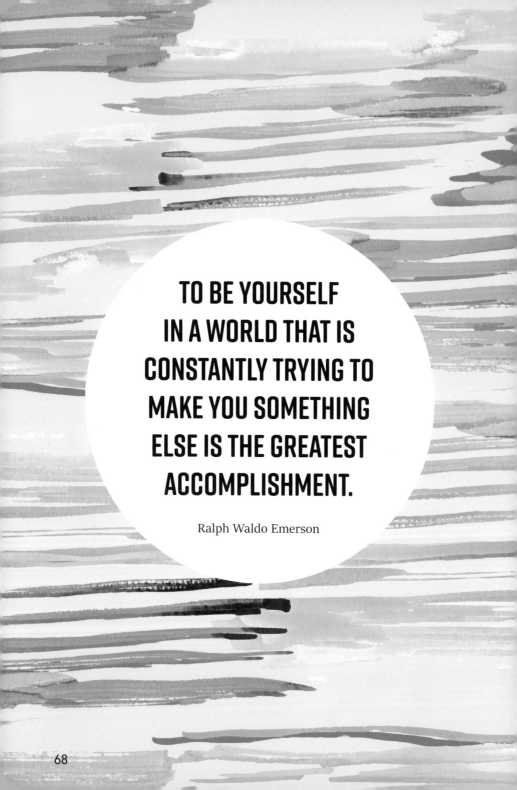

TO BE YOURSELF
IN A WORLD THAT IS
CONSTANTLY TRYING TO
MAKE YOU SOMETHING
ELSE IS THE GREATEST
ACCOMPLISHMENT.

Ralph Waldo Emerson

Make your "I am enough" list

Put to bed your to-do list and, instead, write a list of times when you've felt good enough – times when you've felt confident and your inner critic was quiet. Try to think beyond times when you looked good but of times when you felt great too.

Hold onto the list, keep adding more positive memories to it and refer back to it when your perfectionism is creeping in.

Don't let perfect limit you

Perfectionism can be limiting. We've worked our butts off to meet our sky-high standards, but where to next? Perfect doesn't leave any room for growth and often once people achieve their interpretation of "perfection", it still doesn't feel like enough and they end up putting more and more unrealistic expectations on themselves.

Perfect suggests a finished article but life is all about change. It's about growing, adapting, learning, improving and finding your right path.

The truth is you shouldn't be limited to perfect when you're capable of so much. Stop thinking about just "achieving" or "being better" and consider where and how you'd like to grow in your life.

- What would you like to know more about?
- What would you like to change about where you're currently at in life?
- What's your desired state?
- How can you get there? What do you need to do?

And always, always remember that you are already whole. Growth should be about enhancing what you already have, not completely redefining yourself.

IF EVERYONE'S
CHASING
PERFECTION,
IMAGINE HOW
BORING IT
MUST BE.

why settle for perfect?

YOU PROBABLY WOULDN'T WORRY ABOUT WHAT PEOPLE THINK OF YOU IF YOU COULD KNOW HOW SELDOM THEY DO!

Olin Miller

Find your happy place and switch off

In a world where we're constantly connected to others' lives, it's so important to take time to switch off. Have a think about a place where you feel truly content – somewhere you can unwind and feel at ease – and when things are feeling overwhelming, head there and switch off. Leave your phone behind, have a read, treat yourself to a cake, do whatever makes you feel good. Just enjoy some time for you.

You can
be the ripest,
juiciest peach in the
world and there's still
going to be somebody
who hates peaches.

Dita Von Teese

BE YOU & DO YOU + YOU FOR YOU

JUST BE YOURSELF.
LET PEOPLE SEE THE REAL,
IMPERFECT, FLAWED,
QUIRKY, WEIRD, BEAUTIFUL
AND MAGICAL PERSON
THAT YOU ARE.

Mandy Hale

Focus on what you can change – not what you can't

In life, we often get caught up on things that we have no control over whatsoever. These worries can eat away at us and consume so much of our time that we lose sight of things we can change or control. Generally, you can control what you do but not how people treat you. Once you start shifting your focus in this way, you start worrying a lot less.

Things you can control

- What you eat
- How much exercise you do
- The compliments you give out
- How much time you spend watching TV
- Whether you ask for help

Things you can't control

- Change
- The past
- What people post on Instagram
- What goes on in other people's minds
- When people respond to your WhatsApp messages

Here's a little exercise to help you work out what's within your control and what's not in any situation:

1. Think of a situation in your life that's troubling you or has previously worried you. Jot down a brief outline of it.

2. Make a list of all the things you can control in the situation.

3. Make a list of all the things you can't control in the situation.

4. Identify where you're focusing most of your energy and attention at the moment.

5. Now, from the can control list, circle where you're going to focus your energy from now on.

You deserve every good thing that happens in your life – and more.

**You have been criticizing yourself
for years and it hasn't worked.
Try approving of yourself
and see what happens.**

Louise L. Hay

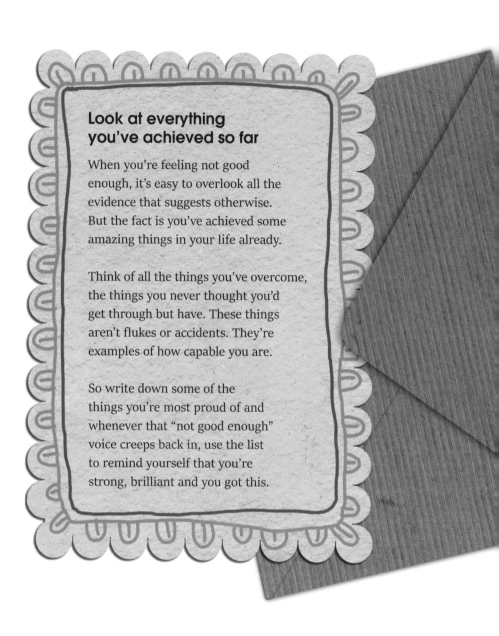

Look at everything you've achieved so far

When you're feeling not good enough, it's easy to overlook all the evidence that suggests otherwise. But the fact is you've achieved some amazing things in your life already.

Think of all the things you've overcome, the things you never thought you'd get through but have. These things aren't flukes or accidents. They're examples of how capable you are.

So write down some of the things you're most proud of and whenever that "not good enough" voice creeps back in, use the list to remind yourself that you're strong, brilliant and you got this.

THE CHANCES ARE THERE WILL ALWAYS BE SOMEONE WHO CAN'T SEE YOUR WORTH. JUST DON'T LET IT BE YOU.

ON

OFF

Part three:

Accepting your unique self and learning to love you

Self-love and self-care – two phrases that are everywhere today. And they're undoubtedly important. But if you've spent years feeling like you're not good enough or constantly trying to be perfect, it's hard to just flick a switch and start loving yourself exactly as you are. This book isn't here to pretend that self-acceptance is something that happens overnight. It's an ongoing journey, not a sprint, but one that's a hundred million per cent worth it.

Throughout this chapter, you'll find some inspiration and innovations to help you see yourself through the light that others see you – and love yourself a little more.

Celebrate your superpower strengths

What's your superpower? I don't mean being able to run through walls or see into the future – but you have some amazing strengths within you and, too much of the time, they are overshadowed by focusing on our weaknesses.

So, let's change that. Right now. Grab a pen and write down a list of all the things that you're good at. They could be the little (but admirable) things like your bad-ass karaoke skills or bigger things like how you always find the strength to bounce back from hard times. It might feel a little unnatural at first, because we're better at picking out our weaknesses than looking at our strengths, but stick with it! And if you struggle, ask a friend to help you out.

Be thankful for what you have;
you'll end up having more.

If you concentrate on what you don't have, you will never ever have enough.

Oprah Winfrey

Less fight or flight, more self-love

Self-compassion guru Paul Gilbert has found that our brains have three different emotional regulation systems which we flit between to manage what we do and how we feel.

The first two are the powerful threat and drive systems. The threat system is the fight or flight mode that comes into play to protect us but can also lead us to overthink and panic. The drive system, which relates to perfectionism, is the system that motivates us towards the things we want (like a new job, a better car, more money, fitness goals).

In moderation, both of these systems have positive qualities. But if our brains spend too much time in either one, our mental well-being can suffer. For example, spending excessive time in our drive system can lead to addiction, burnout, stress, greed and being too hard on ourselves. Whereas, being too tuned in to our threat system can result in anxiety, worry and distress.

The best way to keep our drive and threat system in check is to tap into our third system: the soothing system. This system is all about being content – not seeking, striving or worrying about what we don't have – and embracing the here-and-now. Over the coming pages, we'll look at some hints and tips to help you feel calm, be content with what you have and show yourself some well-deserved compassion rather than criticism.

Self-love.
Self-care.
Self-worth.

There's a reason they all start with self:
you can't find them in anyone else.

JUST FOR A MINUTE: STOP. STOP TICKING OFF YOUR TO-DO LIST. STOP WORRYING WHAT OTHERS ARE THINKING.

STOP AND THINK: WHAT DO I NEED RIGHT NOW?

Unlike self-criticism,
which asks if you're
good enough, self-
compassion asks
what's good for you?

Kristin Neff

Schedule a self-love day

How much of your to-do list is dedicated to you? Probably not enough. Having time for yourself is so important, so put some time for self-love in the diary every week. This could be something super simple: like having a relaxing bath, reading a book or getting an early night, or it could be going to the cinema or treating yourself to a massage. The important thing is that it's time to be good to yourself. You deserve it, big time.

You don't have to change yourself to be loved because you already are – just as you are.

The
mirror
is the
worst
judge
of true
beauty.

The
mirror
is the
worst
judge
of true
beauty.

Sophia Nam

Know you're not alone

When everything looks glossy and filter-fabulous, it's easy to lose sight of reality. But the fact is: everyone struggles sometimes. Everyone experiences pain, everyone makes mistakes, everyone gets spots (however well they hide them). No one's perfect, so don't feel that you have to keep up appearances 24/7. You're only human – just like everyone else.

Today, focus on what is possible.

Learn to let go

If you're anywhere near as sensitive as me, letting go of painful stuff won't come naturally. But holding on to pain and people's wrongdoing is only really hurting one person and that's you. You can spend all of your mental energy feeling angry, disappointed and upset that things didn't work out perfectly, or thinking about what shoulda, woulda, coulda happened, but that energy is wasted. You cannot change what happens to you – only how you react to it.

So learn to let go of things that hurt you, no longer serve you or make you question your worth.

Those models you follow on Instagram that only make you feel bad about yourself? Unfollow them. That ex who broke your heart? Let go of resentment and see the experience as a reminder of what you want/don't want from a relationship.

It is human nature to hold on to things but believe me, there is a beautiful sense of release in letting go of things that weigh heavily on your heart. What's more, it gives you more time and space to focus on the things that matter – things that bring you happiness, joy and self-love.

Think about what you want, not what you're not

Sometimes, we get so focused on what we think we're not that we overlook what it is that we really want. So, try flipping things on their head. Instead of telling yourself that you're not good enough or too much of something, ask yourself: what do I want to be/do instead? This will help you focus on positive actions and goals rather than the negative self-talk that only makes you feel worse.

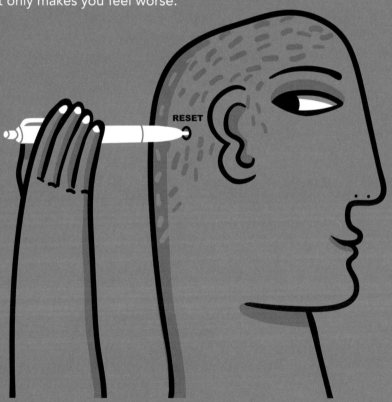

Always be a first-rate version of yourself, instead of a second-rate version of somebody else.

Judy Garland

DON'T YOU DARE, FOR ONE MORE SECOND, SURROUND YOURSELF WITH PEOPLE WHO ARE NOT AWARE OF THE GREATNESS THAT YOU ARE.

Jo Blackwell-Preston

Craft your vision

Creating your very own vision board is a great way of focusing on what you want, rather than someone else's idea of perfection. Here are some pointers to get yours off to a great start:

❶ Set your intentions

❷ What does your life look like in the future? What do you want and how do you want to feel?

❸ Gather your inspiration

❹ Once you've thought about what it is you want to visualize, start gathering pictures, words and things that represent what you want in your life.

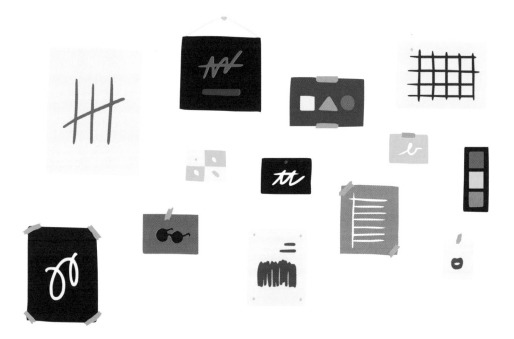

5 Get creative

6 Using corkboard, foam board or a large piece of card as a base, start sticking down your images, words and inspiration. Be as creative as you want – it's your board, after all. Add glitter, colours, texture – whatever helps represent where you want to be and how you want to feel in your future.

7 Manifest your vision

8 Making your vision board is just the first step. Once that's sorted, you can use it to really visualize what you want. Put your board in a place where you can see it every day and spend time remembering what you put on it and why. Use it to influence the decisions and choices you make in your life – and notice the difference it makes.

IF ANYONE TRIES TO MAKE YOU
FEEL LIKE YOU'RE NOT GOOD
ENOUGH, SMILE AT THEM.

REALLY, LOOK THEM RIGHT
IN THE EYES AND SMILE.

THEY DON'T DESERVE YOUR SELF-DOUBT, SADNESS OR WORRY.

AND YOUR SMILE IS WAY TOO BEAUTIFUL TO LET ANYONE TAKE IT AWAY.

Obsess about the good stuff for a change

How long do you spend obsessing about the things that aren't going so well and worrying about what might happen or what's been and gone? As humans, we tend to attach ourselves to things that aren't going great or that we don't like about ourselves. This creates patterns in our minds, and our brains get used to picking up on the negatives over positives.

Noticing the good can dramatically change the way we perceive ourselves. So next time you find yourself feeling "meh", think of the last thing that made you smile and hold that thought!

You is smart.
You is kind.
You is important.

Aibileen Clark in *The Help* by Kathryn Stockett

Swap your inner critic for your inner advocate

You Got This

No really, you have.

You just don't tell yourself it
enough because you're so used
to being hard on yourself.
But look at everything you've achieved.
You've dealt with some real hardships
and bounced back every time.

So swap your inner critic for your
inner cheerleader and instead of
beating yourself up, cheer yourself
on a little more. Go you!

Make peace with the past; it's over.

The future is yours to create.

Have a laugh

When it comes to de-stressing and embracing imperfection, laughter really is the best medicine. It's so powerful, in fact, that a number of hospitals are offering laughter therapies and laughter yoga is deemed to be the next big thing. Having a good laugh is proven to relax us and lift our spirits, as well as a whole host of other health and well-being benefits.

- Research has found that laughter can boost our immune system, by encouraging the flow of super-protective lymphatic fluid and getting lymphocytes circulating in our blood. Clever, huh?

- Laughing is also proven to help us make social connections. I mean, you only have to look at someone who's laughing and try to keep a straight face to see how that can happen.

- Did you know laughing can also help tone your abs? When we laugh, our tummy muscles expand and contract – the same as when we exercise our abs. Who needs sit-ups?

- Laughing for 10–15 minutes can burn up to 40 calories – the same as a cup of salted popcorn. You're welcome.

So make sure you have a laugh every day – doctor's orders.

When you fully appreciate what you bring to the table, you won't be afraid to eat alone.

Change your tune

I'm not good enough. I can't do
that. They won't like me.

We all have tracks that play on repeat in our
minds. But think about it: how well have
they served you so far? To fast-forward from
past mindsets and live more positively, we
need to replace the negative verses we tell
ourselves again and again with kinder ones.

The first step toward doing this is
awareness. So tune in carefully and listen
out for those unhelpful tracks you're telling
yourself. When you notice them, press
stop and try a new, more compassionate
tune. It really does make a difference.

Remember it's not black and white

Life isn't just good or bad, perfect or imperfect. It's a roller coaster of ups and downs, highs and lows, twists and turns. So if things aren't going super smoothly, don't beat yourself up. Trust your journey. Bounce back from setbacks. Find little glimmers of sunshine on dark days. Most importantly, believe in your wonderful self.

No amount of
self-improvement can
make up for any lack
of self-acceptance.

Robert Holden

Mirror, mirror on the wall

When you look in the mirror, instead of picking out your flaws, notice something you like about yourself. Your kind eyes? Your smile? Your favourite feature? Even if you find just one thing, appreciate it – however big or small. Don't let insecurity drown out your unique beauty.

YOU ARE NOT FAT.
YOU HAVE FAT.
YOU ALSO HAVE TOENAILS.
YOU ARE NOT TOENAILS.

You're a goal-smashing survivor!

Think of all the things you've overcome in your life – all those hardships and moments that knocked you yet here you are now, breathing, living, thriving. You survived.

Once we've reached our destinations, we often don't think back about the hurdles we went through to get there but it's important not to overlook how much you've achieved and the challenges you overcame along the way.

So, take a little bit of time to look back at the goals you've achieved. Jot them down, keep them close and keep adding to that list as a reminder of how resilient, brave and downright freaking awesome you are.

Part four:
Living life perfectly imperfectly

We've covered why perfect ain't a thing, how to overcome not feeling good enough and ways to introduce more self-love into our lives. Now, let's talk about how we put all of this into practice.

This chapter is all about tips, tricks and takeaways to help you do your thang, live your truth and break free from the big P.

DON'T WAIT FOR EVERYTHING TO BE PERFECT BEFORE YOU DECIDE TO ENJOY YOUR LIFE.

Joyce Meyer

Forgot those ifs and whens

Chasing perfection is kind of like waiting for a bus to come in the middle of the ocean. It's a recipe for disappointment. But so often, we put all of our focus on ifs and whens. You know the kind... "When I lose weight, I'll be happy" or "If I get this job, everything will be better".

The "I'll be happy when _____" mindset is a pretty common phenomenon but it's a dangerous one. By constantly chasing X, Y or Z in order to feel happy or accomplished, you're not giving yourself a chance to feel content with what you have now. What's more, you're putting your fate in the hands of things you don't necessarily have full control over.

Take being single for instance (my pop quiz subject): people are forever asking you when you're going to meet someone or if you've been on any dates. Then, when you do meet someone, the questioning turns to "<u>When</u> are you getting engaged/married, buying a house or having kids?" And then what? Retirement? Pensions?

Life is about so much more than your next when. It's about what. What makes you happy? What inspires you? What makes you get out of bed in the morning with a smile on your face without snoozing your alarm? And if you don't find those things now, chances are you won't be truly happy when (and if) the next milestone comes along.

So, swap out your whens and look at all the reasons you have to be happy right now.

We need to talk about social media

Ever scrolled through your insta-feed – the bronzed bodies, five-star holidays, engagements, sparkling interiors – and felt deflated? If so, you're not alone. Behavioural scientist Clarissa Silva found that over 60 per cent of people believe that social media has a negative impact on their self-esteem. And it's easy to see why. With over 95 million photos posted on Instagram every single day, it's no wonder we can find ourselves suffering from "compare despair".

For all its good points – cat memes, inspiration, important news and reminders of your pals' birthdays – social media isn't perfect. If we let it, this 24/7 window into others' lives can make us feel deflated or pressured to look, dress, act or even eat a certain way.

The important thing to remember is that nothing shared on social media defines your worth. Fundamentally, does it really matter that a reality TV star is tanning on their eighth beach holiday to Dubai? Or that so-and-so has a new Rolex? Their path is not yours. And every minute spent dwelling on what someone else is doing in their life is time that could be spent focusing on you and the things that truly matter.

one reason we struggle with
insecurity: we're comparing
our behind-the-scenes to
everyone else's highlight reel.

Steven Furtick

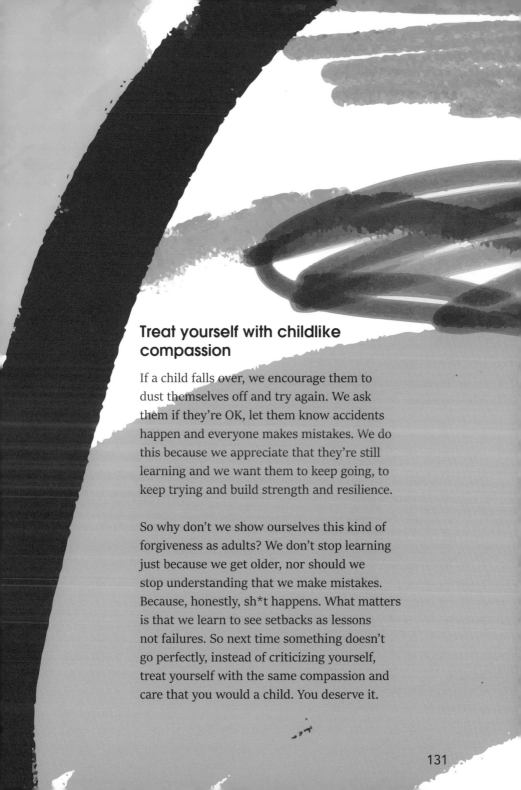

Treat yourself with childlike compassion

If a child falls over, we encourage them to dust themselves off and try again. We ask them if they're OK, let them know accidents happen and everyone makes mistakes. We do this because we appreciate that they're still learning and we want them to keep going, to keep trying and build strength and resilience.

So why don't we show ourselves this kind of forgiveness as adults? We don't stop learning just because we get older, nor should we stop understanding that we make mistakes. Because, honestly, sh*t happens. What matters is that we learn to see setbacks as lessons not failures. So next time something doesn't go perfectly, instead of criticizing yourself, treat yourself with the same compassion and care that you would a child. You deserve it.

Reframe your flaws

Unicorns are great, but humans are freaking incredible. Those things you call your flaws – chances are, they're pretty special. Stretch marks? Try evidence of having epic curves. Visible veins? Proof that blood is healthily pumping through your body, keeping you full of life. Scars? A reminder that you're a total warrior and super survivor. See, those things you call imperfections are pretty awesome after all.

YOUR IMPERFECTIONS ARE MARKS OF AUTHENTICITY,
AND THAT IS THE BEAUTY OF YOU.

Isaac Fowler

Perfection is a subjective myth.

Remember: you cannot read others' minds

When our self-esteem is lacking, we often worry about what others think of us. This happens because we're subconsciously looking for external validation, but it can cause us issues for a number of reasons:

- We can't read minds – and, believe it or not, people think about you a lot less than you might think (probably because they're also busy worrying about what you think of them)!

- It's kind of irrelevant. Everybody thinks and feels differently about things (ahem, Marmite) and not everybody is going to like us. The most important thing you can do to influence how people see you is to be yourself. If they like you, great. If not, you've been authentic and that's what matters.

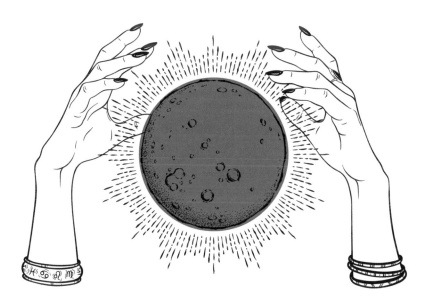

LOVE YOURSELF ENOUGH TO SET
BOUNDARIES. YOUR TIME AND
ENERGY ARE PRECIOUS. YOU GET
TO CHOOSE HOW YOU USE IT.

Anna Taylor

Things you don't always have to do:

- Be an overachiever
- Go the extra mile
- Go above and beyond

Achieving, in itself, is a great accomplishment.

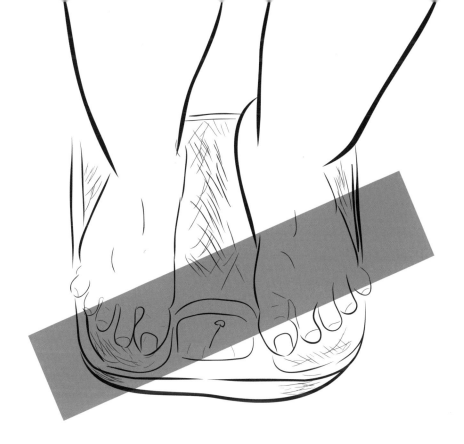

Less meh, more yeah!

It sounds simple but one of the best ways to feel good is to do less of the things that make you feel rubbish. For example, the scales. Your weight fluctuates daily so do not let a number on an electronic machine determine how you feel about yourself. Also, social media – if it's a key source of sadness in your life, reduce your time on it (there are some awesome apps/phone features to help you with this).

Do more of the things that make you feel "YEAH!" and less of those that make you feel "meh".

Focus on living purposefully, rather than perfectly

So now we've established that there's no such thing as a perfect life, where do you focus all those efforts?

Rather than thinking about perfection, focus on your life's purpose. What does a fulfilling life look like to you? What do you value and what really matters? Life isn't just consuming oxygen and breathing out CO_2. So, start focusing on the things you want and need in your life, rather than the things you feel you should and have to do. This alone can change your whole perspective.

When it comes to purposeful living, small steps can make a big difference.

1 Start small.

2 Goals are good but you don't have to achieve them all tomorrow. Making baby steps is more important than rushing ahead and being exhausted when you get there.

3 Ask "why" more.

4 Question why you're doing what you're doing. Is that thing in your diary because it's something you want to do or something you feel you have to do?

5 Stop trying to do it all.

6 Try not to split your energy across too many things (you're only one human!). Instead, take the time to fully focus on what means most to you.

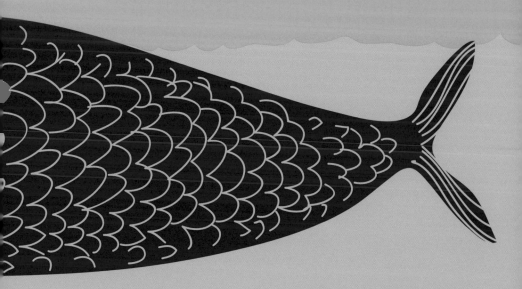

Five questions to help you focus on purpose over perfect

We spend so much time following trends, keeping up appearances and doing things for other people, but how much time are you investing in the things that matter to you? These questions are designed to help you focus on what fulfils you so you can do more of what you love.

❶ What makes you truly happy?

❷ What would you like more of in life?

❸ Aside from material items, what do you value most?

❹ What makes you feel less stressed and more present?

❺ How do you want to be remembered?

Living a purposeful life is about owning your own story, finding your passions and abandoning plans you feel you have to follow. It's about you, your values, hopes, wants and needs. So take note of your answers and start doing more of what fulfils you. Your future self will thank you for it.

FREE FROM "SHOULDS", YOU ARE LIBERATED TO EXPRESS YOURSELF MOST CREATIVELY IN THE MOMENT.

Nick Seneca Jankel

Stop brushing off compliments

Next time someone springs a compliment on you, take it. Thank them, appreciate it and keep reminding yourself of it. Because, do you know what? People don't generally throw compliments around for the heck of it. It's an indication that they've noticed the greatness in you. So listen, instead of dismissing them, and let it sink in to your psyche – because it's the truth!

Realize that life is too short to live by someone else's standards

You were not put on this Earth to please other people. Nor were you put on this Earth to look like magazine models or insta "influencers". You were put on this Earth to live.

Trying to keep up with social pressures or meet others' standards is like chasing a constantly moving target. So, stop following, start owning. Set your own standards. Start thinking about what you want – not what others are doing, wearing or achieving.

Life begins when you shake off the shackles of external expectations and start living for you. Otherwise, you're putting all the power in other people's hands and letting them decide whether you're good enough or not. That's no one's call to make but yours.

You do not need to edit yourself so be you and don't look back – you're not going that way.

THAT WAS THE DAY
SHE MADE HERSELF THE
PROMISE TO LIVE MORE
FROM INTENTION AND
LESS FROM HABIT.

Amy Rubin Flett

SOMETIMES BOX SQUATS,

SOMETIMES BOX SETS.

IT'S ABOUT BALANCE.

Make sure your mind and soul are getting as much exercise as your butt and abs.

Get comfortable saying "no"

When you're always saying "yes" to everything, you can quickly end up spreading yourself too thinly. So, use your yeses wisely and don't be afraid to say no when you need to.

I, for one, used to be a real yes woman. Could you just pick up that meeting? Yep. Can you help me with this thing? Sure. I'd say yes to things without a second thought and end up drowning under the pressure. Not only is it logistically hard to manage but it's a fast route to burnout too.

You don't owe everyone a yes but you do owe yourself the time to recharge and rejuvenate. So, start saying no more often. See your hours in the day like currency and be mindful with how you spend them. Don't let other people or shoulds determine your entire to-do list or diary and be more decisive about what's worth your time and what isn't.

Every time you say no, you're simply taking control of your life rather than letting someone else dictate it. There's nothing wrong with that whatsoever.

Focus on what you have, not what you haven't

Sure, you may not have everything you want in life but most
of us have what we need right now to move forward.

When you separate out what you want from what you need,
you start to see things differently and live more freely.

So, stop thinking about what you haven't got
and start considering all the amazing things
that you have in your life at the moment.

Action : Jot down all the good things in your
life right now – and keep adding to the list.

Don't worry, be *wabi-sabi*

In Japanese culture, *wabi-sabi* is a way of living that focuses on appreciating things as they are, seeing beauty in imperfections and making the most of life. It's all about peacefully accepting that things change and flux. Instead of dwelling on difficulties, it encourages noticing the blessings in daily life.

Next time you're plagued with imperfect thoughts, think wabi-sabi, smile and enjoy the little wonders of your day.

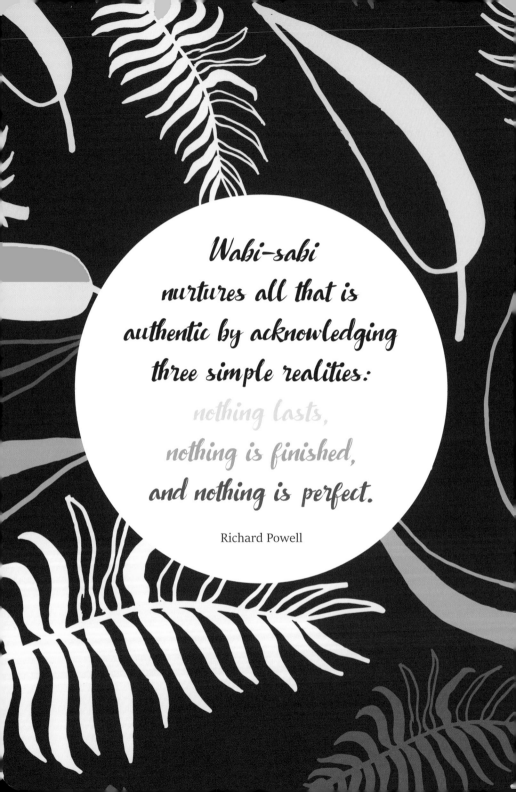

Wabi-sabi nurtures all that is authentic by acknowledging three simple realities: nothing lasts, nothing is finished, and nothing is perfect.

Richard Powell

Conclusion:
Goodbye perfection, hello freedom

The end of this book marks the start of your new chapter and the beginning of your perfectly imperfect life. Free from the impossible-to-reach, moving target of "perfection", it's time to embrace all the wonders of you and start living your awesomely authentic self.

This is your story – and this is just the beginning.

AND NOW
THAT YOU
DON'T HAVE
TO BE
PERFECT,
YOU CAN
BE GOOD.

John Steinbeck

Image credits

If you're interested in finding out more about our
books, find us on Facebook at **Summersdale Publishers**
and follow us on Twitter at **@Summersdale**.

WWW.SUMMERSDALE.COM